KU-221-861

ROLLING STONES VOODOO LOUNGE

STRIPPED

PHOTOGRAPHIC CREDITS

FRONT & BACK COVER: Duncan Raban © ALL ACTION

© ALL ACTION Pages: 3, 6, 4, 14, 16, 19, 22, 28, 30, 37, 54-57, 63-71, 78

© REX FEATURES Page: 29

© GUNNAR SKIBSHOLT Pages: 12, 15, 20-25, 27, 31-53, 58-61, 72-80

Copyright © 1995 UFO MUSIC BOOKS LTD

All rights reserved. Printed in Great Britain. No part of this book may be used or reproduced in any manner whatsoever without written permission except in the case of brief quotations embodied in critical articles or reviews.

For more information write to;
UFO Music, 18 Hanway Street, London W1P 9DD, England
Telephone: 0171 636 1281   Fax: 0171 636 0738

First published in Great Britain 1995
UFO Music Ltd, 18 Hanway Street,
London W1P 9DD

The author and publishers have made every effort to contact all copyright holders. Anyone who for any reason have not been contacted are invited to write to the publishers so that a full acknowledgment may be made in subsequent editions of this work.

ISBN 1-873884-41-9

Designed by UFO Music Ltd

Printed by BUTLER & TANNER Ltd. Frome and London

ROLLING STONES
VOODOO LOUNGE

STRIPPED

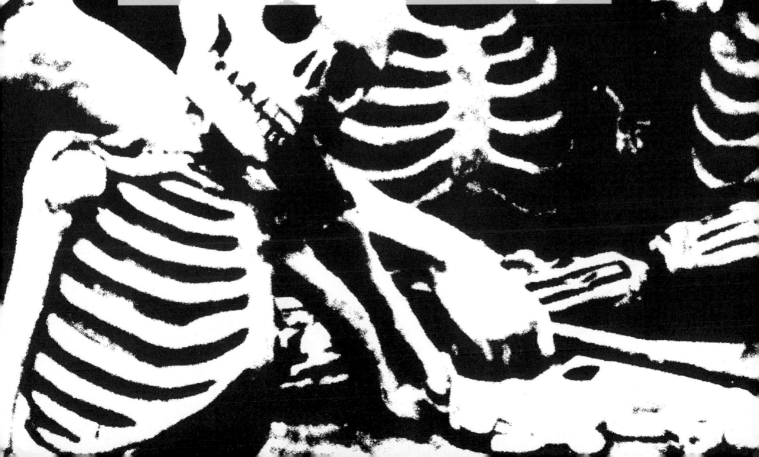

foreword

Mr Gunnar Skibsholt is a dentist by day and a photographer by night filling in the gaps other photographers leave behind. The bulk of the live photographs in this book were taken with his 300mm telephoto lens attached to his Nikon camera, using Simon's (his tall son) shoulders as a tripod to steady the camera. Not only has Mr Skibsholt extracted great live photographs, but he is also one of the few gentlemen to have witnessed the Stones' very first concert in Denmark in 1965. A true fan, a true dentist and a great bloke.

Dave Hogan is the fortunate man responsible for the marvellous shots of the Toronto debut show as well as being one of only two official photographers to be allocated photographic passes for the infamous Brixton Academy show in London, along with Justin Thomas.

Many of the interviews featured in this book were conducted by Westwood One and we send our thanks to Joe Garner.

A big thankyou to our overwhelmed designer Mike Edgar and the ever patient Acrelda and Zi, Mike Koshitani, Yuji Ikeda, Jordi Tarda, Sean Lees for use of the word 'Stubbies' (beer), Alessandro Locchi, Stephen Shepphard to name but a few.

FOCUS

The Rolling Stones last recorded work *'Steel Wheels'* was the end of a long relationship with CBS records subsequently the label lost direction after being bought out by the Japanese firm Sony. True to form the Stones embarked on the World's most successful tour the *'Steel Wheels and Urban Jungle Tour'* ending in 1990. The tour was hailed as a success by all spectators and the media alike. The tour was followed by forays into the solo career world by the individual Stones, a prelude of what was to come. Signed to a new label, the infamous Virgin Records, it was rumoured that Branson signed the Stones to make it a more attractive proposition for when he actually sold the label to recording giant EMI Records. The first LP recorded for Virgin had to surpass anything the Stones had previously undertaken. As they had been christened the *'Greatest Rock 'n' Roll Band in the World'* back in 1969 they wanted to be able to fulfil this prophecy. And fulfil it they did with their strongest recorded album since *'Black and Blue'*.

The *'Voodoo Lounge'* has a warmer soulful sound than the previous rockier *'Steel Wheels'* LP- with plenty of thought behind the song writing. Keith Richards and Mick Jagger on friendlier terms than on the last LP also had the input of rock's smartest dressed man Charlie Watts. Supported by a new bass player and a horn section led by Bobby Keys, the Stones were set to take on the world again with a more soulful element to the band.

From every Stones LP seems to come a rock classic *'Start Me Up'* from the *'Tattoo You'* album is at present being used to promote Bill Gates' new Windows 95 programme in the UK.

Left: Keith concentrates at a secret concert at Bagley's Warehouse, London, on September 21st 1995 to promote their latest album *'Stripped'*.

'I Go Wild' is one of the rock classics from the Voodoo Lounge album proving to be a firm favourite on this tour. Mick and Keith talk about how the album came together and their own thoughts on the album.

Mick Jagger *Yeah! It sounds good, yeah it's a warmer sound that's the idea and that's the fashion, four years ago the fashion was to be more slick, now it's not. I just subscribe it all to fashion.*

The song writing techniques of Mick and Keith are legendary. Songs can be written in five minutes while coping with an exhausting schedule on tour but once a songwriter has real time to come up with ideas the results can be more rewarding.

Mick Jagger *The trick with lyrics, Keith gives me some help with some of the ideas, with phrases like 'sparks will fly' and you're off. Its better than nothing and it gets you going and we write it down when an idea comes to us early on, otherwise you just end up with titles that don't get you anywhere. So as soon as the thing comes up you try and get some ideas for it so I just write them down quickly and then I go back and revise them. I had time with this record to do that. On the Steel Wheels, I didn't have enough time to revise because it was all a bit of a rush. So I go back and say that first verse is great but, the politics of song writing are the first verse has to be really good to grab attention. So you might write a fantastic third verse and decide it could be the first. When your revising for example say in a song like 'You Got Me Rockin', I don't know what I wrote but say I wrote "I was a butcher cutting up meat" in the third verse, I'd think I really like that line and it's good one to open up with, so you start re-arranging, that's the craft aspect of it so to speak. The other thing is that I've seen so many aspiring writers labouring over rhyming like 'Your Love Is Strong', just write what comes into your head on a particular idea, and then your off. Then you've got pages of this stuff which doesn't rhyme later but if you're slaving over rhymes your brain doesn't unload it. I just watch people tear their hair out, there's ideas there and all they do is write in rhymes.*

Thirty years after being locked in a kitchen to write their first song, they've returned to do the same.

Mick Jagger   *We did the same this time, we sat down in my kitchen and talked about what kind of LP we wanted to make and what we didn't want to make. So we had a bit of a chat about it this time which is good, we didn't want to make a totally rock n' roll album only concentrating on rock. We didn't want to leave out little odd things that we would have considered years ago saying how average they were, I'm thinking of "Moon Is Up" , "New Faces". On this new stuff we wanted to keep it more straight forward and direct and then we talked about the rhythmic structure, which Charlie and I did a lot of work on, but we didn't use a lot in the end, so that was something that didn't happen. But this LP was pretty much thought out.*

Keith Richards   *We did sit around in Mick's kitchen in February 1993, all I can remember was we were kickin' ideas around and talking and I came out with one word "focus". We would have to get some good grooves down, we were talking musically first but really my mind came out with focus. We'd all be looking down the same scope, we've all got the others ingredients all we need to do is focus. It was one of those magical things finding Don Was, Mick and I knew we both needed somebody because we couldn't take on the whole task ourselves. If you keep making records two or three in a row you can do it but we knew this was a very important record for the Stones. We had to make a record that we liked not that we don't always for instance Steel Wheel, I was just happy to make it. The fact that we were physically making it and we did it very quickly and it was very successful, competently it was very good but for me it was like the beginning, it was almost a rebirth, were all acting like babies again.*

Keith Richards talking about *'Out Of Tears'* and how the title for the album was conceived.

It's got the feel on it, that extra indefinable ingredient that nobody can muster up, you can't just pop your fingers and say give me the magic ingredient, but this one has it.

I was in Barbados with Mick and Charlie at Eddie Grants Studio, which is on his estate, this is where we stayed. This is also where Eddie lives with his wife, and two hundred cats that live on the grounds of the estate. Anyway there's a lot of land and Eddie has three studios on the estate. One night I was going from the house to the studio, it was a real tropical evening, thunderstorms, rain, I was in a plastic sheet running to get to the Studio and it's night time. I saw this animal standing in the corner and it was a small cat, so I tried to put him back with his mother but the cat was the runt of the litter so was rejected. So I picked it up and took it to the studio and said this cat is 'voodoo'. Whenever I work I have a sign up on my amps saying 'Docs Office' (I have many names in the business) and I decorate it with scarves and that's my territory, I like that you know. You should see my room, I immediately decorate everything to make it personal. Anyway so I had this sign Doc's office and then I added in my head 'Docs office and Voodoo Lounge, so it was with us all the way when we were writing the songs, from Ireland to LA even when there was an earthquake and we'd finished the album the sign was still there. Mick and I looked at each other for a title and after writing 150 songs, I'm all out of titles. The record company were yelling at us for a title as they already had a release date, Mick suddenly turned around and looked at the sign above my amplifier and said what about the 'Voodoo Lounge', that's why the cat in Barbados became the most famous cat in the whole world. And the p.s. to all of that is, they let me take the cat to the US and now she's got three kittens living in Connecticut and is doing very well.

Keith comments if a hit song is easy to write.

Keith Richards

Sometimes it works and sometimes it doesn't. 'Love Is Strong' for instance, you start playing it, like it and immediately start singing it up, it's forceful. I've got a little cassette of when we first wrote it and it was an octave lower, which Mick has very rarely done. It's a hard place for a singer to be because you get used to using all your force and if you're not using it in that way, you can get very nervous singing down low. But he got into it and persevered with it and suddenly he got it and kept it in the groove. Mick's singing better than I heard him sing in years.
There's no such thing as boredom if you've got a guitar. Sleep is important. I once stayed up for nine days - I gave up doing that because when you do fall asleep it could be anywhere. I fell asleep on top of a speaker once in point nought of a second. Nine days is my record and I'm leaving it that way, it's a lot of fun not sleeping for

two days because you don't need to take anything, you're in another world. I wrote 'Satisfaction' in my sleep, I woke up in the middle of the night and taped it. How did I do it? I played it back in the morning only to find forty five minutes of "Satisfaction" and forty five minutes of me snoring in the middle of it.

The most famous song in the history of rock was conceived while Keith was asleep. Chuck comments on Keith's song writing prowess.

Chuck Leavell   *Keith has this amazing ability to write songs that sound like standards in their melodic content like 'Slippin' Away'. They have a certain chord structure that are unusual but standard, that's what comes from him listening to people like Hoagey Carmichael, he's a big fan of those kinds of writers.*

So with the album recorded and the title of the LP decided, the press and the record buying public alike start to interpret what the songs are about for example whether or not they relate to actual events such as 'New Faces', which is said to be Jagger's psychological assessment of the cult of 'Kurt Cobain' but Jagger denies the claim and he goes on to explain human nature.

Mick Jagger   *You look at a movie or statue and each person has their own interpretation, songs are the same, everything is open to an individuals own interpretation. So if that's their interpretation then fine. When people come to the Voodoo Lounge Show, they say "What do you think that set was?" Some think it was a big dentist's chair, another might say it was a big snake, it's the same with songs.*

NEW FACES

A drastic change occurred before the tour began, Bill Wyman, one of the four original remaining members, had already upset the Stones by opening his *'Sticky Fingers'* restaurant without asking permission for using the name and his well publicised exploits with Mandy Smith had also made Bill Wyman a household name. Bill always threatened to leave the band. This time it became a reality. Thirty one years after joining, the rhythm section line up was to change.

Keith Richards   *When I realised that Bill was actually serious, eventually I had to face up to it that yeah, he does actually mean it and that is a big deal to change your rhythm section after thirty years not many people have the chance to have a rhythm section together after thirty years but it did occur and it was a hell of a deal. So I said to Charlie, "you pick the rhythm". We tried all the best bass players in the world and everybody plays for an hour or so, there's no basis to make up your mind because they are all so good. This is when we first used Charlie as an arbitrator, so we said you choose the rhythm section and he said "You're putting me in the hot seat". Only once in thirty years! Come on Charlie, yes we are putting you in the hot seat and Mick and I played advisers. He plumped for Darryl straight off and he slotted straight in, it was probably one of the better things he did last year and being able to have Charlie prepared to play that part, he's got a whole new thing going, and I'm still trying to figure him out.*

Charlie Watts previously the shy man of the band had gained experience in stating his views, this experience was gained from running his own jazz quartet. When Bill stated he was leaving Charlie wasn't too upset.

Charlie Watts   *No I wasn't because I get on well with Bill, quite well, in fact I spoke to him last week. I know him very well and these are the only times I miss Bill really; when we're not doing anything I go and talk to him. I think he got to a stage in life when he thought to himself I've got 20 years to live and I don't want to spend 2 more of them doing that. I don't think you can argue with that and he was very up front about it. He said it four years ago but we gave him a long time to think about it, two years in fact.*

Ronnie Wood had his own views how the band felt as a whole with Bill's departure.

Ronnie Wood   *We're having a great time without Bill and not missing him at all. He turned up on my birthday, he looked like an accountant, he had all his hair shaved evenly, wearing glasses and an evening suit. I said to Mick have you seen whose over there? Mick did a double take and said "Whose that?" Only Bill I said and he said "No!" He's been with him all his life and he sees him for the first time in two months and he didn't recognise him, he's changed that much. But he's so happy with Suzanne his new wife and he doesn't like to get on planes, that's the main reason he left. He thinks his luck is up, he's been on so many planes and doesn't want to get on any more.*

Enter Darryl Jones who welcomed the challenge playing with the greatest band in the world having played with Miles Davis the greatest improviser in music to date. One of Charlie Watts' many admirers, the thought of playing with Miles Davis' bassist sparked the imagination of Charlie Watts. But Darryl still has to learn the bass notes from the concise history of the Rolling Stones book, putting in his own personal touch.

Darryl Jones

There's a thousand bass players who can play way faster than me, and who know a lot more tricks than I do, I deal with the fundamentals, and I play rock-solid bass. That's what I love to do. I mean, I can dig a solo, if the musical genre is appropriate for it. But that is not my first love. My first love is laying down the bass line, and it's the same thing I did with Herbie Hancock and Miles Davis, and the same thing I'm doing here.

The guys make it a lot of fun to play with them. Watching Keith play the guitar, obviously he's been playing for a long time, he's been listening to a lot of great music and stuff for a long time. At the same time he really does play the guitar with a sense of wonder almost like the kind of excitement of a musician whose just learnt how to play the instrument. So it doesn't sound old when he plays it sounds fresh, it seems he's constantly discovering something new. The best way I can explain it is I can remember when I first learnt how to play a particular song that I really loved, you play it with a kind of excitement and wonder that sometimes gets lost when you've been playing for a long time.

So the man who replaced one of the original members of the band had suddenly become the new boy, thereby lifting the pressure of Ronnie Wood who replaced Mick Taylor way back in 1975.

Ronnie Wood

It's nice not to be the new boy anymore. Darryl is a good man, very quick like you have to be with this lot. I remember June 1st 1975 my birthday, I had one hundred and fifty songs spinning around in my head it was my first live gig with them. I learnt a lesson then that I'll never remember all the chords, just take an average, just gimme the key, eyes down and I'll see you at the end.

SPARKS WILL FLY

With the album recorded with the new boy, preparations were made for what was going to be the world's most successful tour to date, breaking all previous records. One of the reasons for the success is due to the design of the set coupled with the input of the band themselves as well as going to other concerts to check out the competition.

Mick Jagger   *Charlie went to see the Phil Collins show when we were rehearsing in Toronto, but I missed seeing the Pink Floyd show as I was working that night, and I just felt I couldn't miss the rehearsal night. I saw the U2 show and thought it was excellent, that's it really, I did see Michael Jackson's European stage show and that was actually very good, I know he's not really fashionable and people bad mouth him, it was actually quite a good show. I thought he's very hardworking, and I like to see people working the stage, dancing and moving around, it gives it more vibe. It's better than watching the Floyd, because even though I like them they don't move much, but I do think they put on a fantastic light show. When you say am I watching for the competition so to speak, I thought the U2 show was really innovative, but it was still on the curve of the Steel Wheels thing, but it's all designed by the same people.*

Mark Fisher - Designer of the stage set for U2 and Pink Floyd (others present at this time are Mick Jagger, Charlie Watts, Patrick Woodruff).

It maybe the first time where you can sit at the back and have a better seat at this show, you could sit up front and catch the band but you get much more of the entire spectacle if you sit further back, I don't know if that's happened before in a Stadium rock show.

There were some things that were known and they were that they had to set a precedence and did not want to follow what had gone on before. They wanted to find something completely different which more or less meant the antithesis of anything earlier. This more or less gave us a few clues straight away, the most important one was to understand what Steel Wheels actually was, that if it had been this retro end of the world, end of the industrial era, cyberpunk, William Gibson's Blade Runner type image of the end of the world if you like, end of the know industrial universe, the end of things like petroleum refineries, space rockets and things. So this stage set was really for the moment in time, but looking to the future. So whereas that was what had ended this is about what lies ahead, it's the wired gigabyte, internet city but all that stuff is invisible. Whereas you can make a steel mill and everyone can see it for what it is, we had to invent something completely fresh here and say this is our image. That is what we did, we spent a long time playing around and drawing on different sources and from scientific diagrams.

I was trained as an architect but ran away to the circus to avoid having a real job. So it's fantastic to be part of this huge team. On the one hand you're looking at the project from a conceptual point of view, but on the other hand you're part of this very efficient army that's organised to build things, that's very exciting.

Patrick Woodruff

The attraction and strength of working with the Rolling Stones is whatever I do with the lighting, the fireworks the costumes, the videos, special effects as long as I leave them lit in the middle of this enormous structure I'd be all right but I can't do that with many other groups. They have such huge energy, such recognisable faces, such great music when they're on, there is nothing one can do to upstage them. I can think of very few other performers one could say that of because it is very easy to dwarf them with that stuff but on the other hand your forced to do it on such a large scale because if you don't, if you try and do something on a scale which seems comfortable or intimate for the group, you're not really giving anyone their money's worth. It's a really fine balance because there's always been the argument that the Rolling Stones are such a great rock band, you just put them on stage and they'll be great, well it's not true basically for two reasons. Firstly it would get really boring even with the best band in the world, they look like ants from that distance and you're not aware that anything's coming even with the best sound in the world for two and a half hours you'd get bored.

Secondly the Rolling Stones have been about far more than just their music, they are social icons, what they do, who they marry etc. those are all social implications, so there is far more to do with it than just their records and their music. Their show's have always been far better than anyone else's and I am not saying that in a competitive way, the Rolling Stones Stadium shows are always unique.

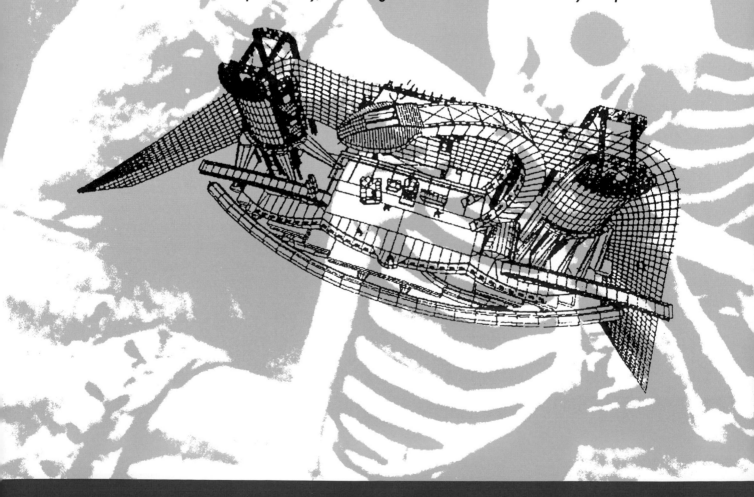

Mick loves all that theatre and he loves different places to go and different props to jump onto, whether its the blow up phallus or climbing up on top of the structure for "Sympathy For The Devil", that's all part of it. Keith is not against all that thing but he's more instinctively focused on just his space and his patch, driving the band playing the music but the great thing about working for both of them is the relationship is not cut and dried. Although Mick loves theatrics, he is keyed into his performance. He is a very disciplined performer and likes to know where he is going. Keith is in his own way very theatrical, he is the personification of rock n' roll. He is a man with an eye, for someone who dresses like that must see the theatre and drama of their performance. He's a good yardstick for me it's easy to run things through Keith and work out if you've got the balance right and Charlie's good for that too.

The set designers came up with the perfect compliment to the Stones. The band surround themselves with true professionals wherever they go, one of them being Lisa Fisher backing singer extraordinaire who brings the house down with her duet on 'Sympathy For The Devil'.

Lisa Fisher

The difference between the Steel Wheels tour and this one, is that there is a lot more love, a lot more give and take and a lot more understanding. Sometimes time is a great healer of all things and so just with any family member that you have things to deal with. I think having the 5 years off and coming back to it, makes you think Steel Wheels was a really great thing, lets make this an amazing thing. I think everybody's heart was in the same place and it was good because everybody was comfortable with each other. Bobby Keys knew me and Bernard, it felt good not to have to worry if someone was going to be stable, or professional, their gonna let me do the job well and really enjoy what their doing. I'm really looking forward to a year of this, at first it was like oh yeah! I'm going to kill myself but when you're having fun and everyone you work with is number one it's not a problem. I worked with Luther Vandross for ten years and I left the Steel Wheels tour to go back to him and then I did the Urban Jungle tour with the Stones, just the similarities between the two are really interesting because Luther also has to have everything number one. So I've really been blessed to have these kind of people in my life.

Ronnie Wood

We're all so different people, from all walks of life, London School of Economics, vocalists, you've got varied Art School people in the rest of the band. But even with the advent of Darryl Jones on the bass, it's no big thing, he's slotted right in and he's a gent. We've got Bernard Fowler, who deserves the best mention anyone can give anyone, Bobby Keys, whose a survivor from the earliest times. Lisa Fisher, who is very overlooked and a wonderful singer and Chuck Leavell the old stalwart. Since we haven't got Stu and Max Ewall and those new west home boys - there good Bobby's little team that he can crack the whip at and everyone is so pleased to be there including us.

With just one more hurdle in their way before starting the tour - the press - the band are ready to rock.

Ronnie Wood

This tour is the most exciting tour, especially since the press would like to think the dinosaurs can't make it. But were still inspired and that youthful bit still drives the music and the presentation. Even when Mick used to say he couldn't see himself singing Satisfaction at forty, this is all old quote stuff now but I still remember him saying it. He didn't think that people would wear it. I don't think at the time you know because then it was unheard of. But now he's fifty and he's better than he's ever been, I think things get better.

Mick Jagger

I just wonder why someone would be so negative before the gigs. I don't think regular people and ticket buyers expected to see the band not do well. I only say that because in the last tour, it was pretty good. We did a good sound and energetic show and everyone seemed to like it. It was very well reviewed and o.k. it was four years ago but we carried on doing it, so why after four years, why should you suddenly not be able to do it anymore. That sort of huge doubt shouldn't be cast on anyone, o.k. if last time we were a bit tired, or off key, a bit lack lustre, but this wasn't reflected in the reviews we got and it wasn't the general opinion of the people that came to see us. If people had said o.k. not again, it was bad enough the last time I can understand it, but that wasn't so. So I kinda think it was a bit of a negative attitude to start saying three and half years later, it's really a hopeless task, it's a bit negative, so getting over that is wonderful.

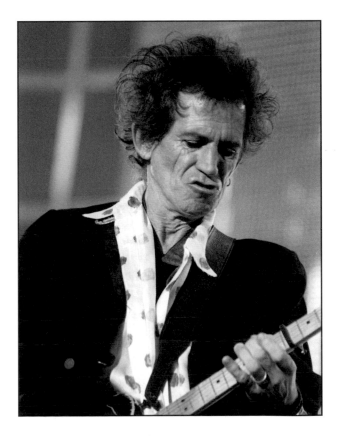

Keith Richards

Every time you go onto the next thing you find yourself more and more under microscopes that you don't really want. But I suppose it is an inevitable thing because nobody has taken it this far down the road yet. Not rock n' roll anyway. To me music is music, you can have any names you like but basically music is music. And if your gonna hit and happen and be fortunate enough to land up in my case with the right bunch of guys, it's a passion and it's a pleasure. Very early on in a way your still the kid sitting at the top of your stairs trying to get down Buddy Holly's latest single, there's still a bit of that in you, because it's always fresh and new, If you're lucky in that way to play with the right guys.

That is the miracle about bands, it's got nothing to do with musicianship perse, it's just got to do with the human chemistry, it's indefinable.

Mick Jagger

Of course you get pompous over 25 years and make remarks you wish you never had, people taking the piss and so on, I think you have to try and remain on an even keel. One of the things I don't like about touring is you don't remain on an even keel, it's inevitable, you just gotta try and keep your feet on the ground and when people tell you how wonderful you are, thousands of people waiting on you and girls taking their tops off all the time. When you've finished it all you just have to come down and be yourself. It's easy to say but a lot of people get carried away with it. That's when the whole thing gets totally out of hand and it isn't fun to be on the road when people get carried away with their own self importance and their own fame, of course I do it. The trouble is you have to have a huge ego to be able to do this in the first place.

Mick admits he has a huge ego but I'm sure any human being who is probably better known by name than Her Majesty the Queen - Elizabeth who? around the world has a right to be egotistical. Ronnie Wood reflected.

I never forgot after the final date on The Steel Wheels/Urban Jungle tour after a couple of years or whatever it was, Keith Mick and I had a ...... celebratory toast in this hotel in London to say we did it you know and it was nice for them to invite me in to say lets have a drink and we did it and I got the impression then that they were enjoying it far too much to say were not touring again, I could see it going on.

START ME UP

The Stones famed for their original tour announcements, the most infamous being the 1975 tour of America. Central Manhattan, New York was brought to a standstill during the day as the Stones played 'Brown Sugar' from the back of an open air truck, driving slowly up Madison Avenue. They actually looked together as a band for the first time since Ronnie Wood joined back in 1975. Ronnie Wood had his own views of the press.

The announcement of the Voodoo Lounge Tour was slightly low key, the press conference was held at the Pier on Manhattan's east side New York. Already differences were manifesting themselves compared to previous tours. The main difference being that the four members of the Stones were to face the press together as opposed to Jagger's solo announcement in London on the Steel Wheels Tour.

Having announced the start of the Voodoo Lounge Tour at a secret concert in a strip joint, Toronto Canada, the Stadium shows, which takes one and a half million watts of power, 1500 lights, the worlds biggest travelling jumbo screen and a lot of pyrotechnics, 510,000 tonnes of steel and the skill and muscle of 250 people and the cost is four ($4,000,000) million dollars, were to start in Washington D.C.. Nerves set in at the thought of facing 70,000 eager spectators and over 1,000 of the worlds press.

Keith Richards

For me a dreadful calm descends on me on the first night, that's my way of dealing with it, watching everyone else running around like headless chickens. I wanna say calm down guys get some of this dreadful calm and then I open the cage and I'm ready. But usually on the first night, you're aware its the first night from the beginning to the very end and then suddenly four or five numbers into the show, I realise I've totally forgotten its the first night. I'm totally at home relaxed and everybody's playing great and it's not like five years have gone by since you've played something or done something on that scale. It's not the playing so much it's like will it work in the Stadium, you never know until the people are in there. We were there all last week in an empty Stadium, it seemed to work and the school gym we rehearse in, it works there too, you never know until the first night if its actually gonna work with the people, their the vital ingredient. My other fear is that your first show goes well and the second one usually falls flat on it's face, it's quite common, but this one didn't, it got better. So everybody's up and its unbelievable!

Mick Jagger

I don't really get apprehensive, but I've got to concentrate, I started to lose my concentration at one place on the second night and I thought am I really doing this or am I dreaming. It's really dangerous but its actually rather nice in a way, it's like being on drugs or something, but you can't lose it, you've gotta concentrate because your in a band and they're playing the same arrangement you see. You can do it on acid you know and you can't do it in a dreamlike state because you might just really lose it.

• START ME UP •

Once the nerves have settled other problems arise such as the vastness of the stage, which can be frustrating especially if you're the drummer.

Charlie Watts   *All I can see is their heads and their bums, because their entertaining the troops you know, I'm just facing that way and no I can't really see anything. There's things that go on over there, and I've got no idea what they are. Not the last tour but the one before I've forgotten the name of it, that was the worst one for what's called sight lines because Mick and Keith would literally disappear, and I wouldn't know where they were. This present stage, they haven't quite got to grips with it yet but once they do they'll be all over it. When Keith goes for a walk and comes back twenty minutes later and that's kinda funny.*

Now the other night when the pyro man lit the lights for the fireworks, they went above my head and burnt holes in all the drums, I don't mean hot burns, they marred all the heads, their made of plastic so these tiny little things come down and that's something you can never really know until you've done it, so they've been moved for the next show, but it just goes to show that that's the sort of thing you can never ever rehearse.

The Stones normally associated with the wasted look, bottle of Jack Daniels in one hand and a cigarette in the other had after years of abuse cleaned up their act. They were professional and were concerned with providing the definitive tour rather than drinking throughout the show, although many of the bottles of Jack Daniels were watered down just before the show without Ronnie or Keith knowing. During the show Keith has more fun these days listening to Ronnie on stage.

Keith Richards   *He just comes up and says things like: I love you, or I hate you or, where did you get that jacket, or I thought that was all right you know or what happens next? I don't know! Those kinds of things, or Mick will come up and say, "What's Ronnie doing"? Or what are you doing? That's the great thing no matter how much you rehearse there's always that element of looseness where the number can always change the whole face of the song and everyone looks at each other and says where did that come from?*

Chuck Leavell also talks about the looseness of the band.

Chuck Leavell   *There's a lot of stories that I can tell you about over the last decade. My memory normally stems from things that happen on stage and there's one example that I remember most vividly. It was the one concerning Blinded By Love, it worked out for the Urban Jungle Tour and the first night we did it. Mick was playing guitar and went out towards the audience, there were 60,000 people out there, he stood and the microphone, he turned around and walked straight up to me and said "What's the first line of the song"? and luckily I remembered it, "The poor princess of Wales" and he said "Oh! God, Thanks!" and those are the ultimate moments that strike me.*

Keith Richards

A band especially one that's been together as long as we have is beyond explanation, its a very special relationship. Sometimes were very cold blooded with each other but you can do that with people who know you.

I've seen Charlie fight his way back through a load of cops just to get his drum sticks. He's an amazing drummer and secondly he's not a volatile personality so when he does express himself - you tend to listen with extra care. He is also a very private person and has always felt slightly embarrassed at being a star, he can never figure it out, not that any of us can either. I don't think he's had any real feelings about his role in the band, not like he does when he's working on his own, he made a beautiful record (From One Charlie - on UFO Music) - he loves to do jazz stuff. But I have noticed that since we started to do the 'Voodoo Lounge Tour' that Charlie has suddenly started to state his case and has become an important ingredient over the last year or so, and this helps to balance things out between Mick and I. Point of views always came from Mick or myself and when we clashed there was nothing to stop us, now we say let's ask Charlie.

I arrived here last Tuesday and found out the stage had fallen down last Sunday, nobody had said anything, so I let off a few salvos that people wouldn't forget but they all came around afterwards and said we needed that, don't moan about things, I just exploded!

Ronnie Wood

I was talking to Keith in the Voodoo Lounge last night early memories, I was sitting there with his dad as well. I was always thought he was from the south of the river. I lived in Hayes and Keef said "Two miles down the road that's where I first discovered Elvis, it changed my life."

When Brian Jones died and they did that concert at Hyde Park and I'm walking around the outskirts of Hyde Park and I bumped into Mick and Charlie and I shook their hand and they said see you soon. We got into what a small world it was and Mick came by my room and gave me a bracelet, my own hat and my own blade saying I think you should be armed now - it was really sweet.

The backing vocalists have their own views of the Glimmer Twins. Although some of their initial nerves were not only on the opening night of the tour.

Bernard Fowler
about Mick Jagger

I said right after the first show, I never give compliments but he blew me away and I said if and when I get to be your age I want to be like that.

Lisa Fisher

I met Keith in a recording studio and everyone was telling me he's really freaked out and out of his mind - I was thinking what's he going to be like? and I was really glad that they asked me to work on the record in London. So I met Sarah Dash and Bernard Fowler, and Keef walks in and says "Heeeey bayyybeeee how yaaa doing?" I realised he meant "How you doing baby"? At first it was OK I better get used to the accent and the gravely sexy voice. So after a while I started to call him "Cookie Monster" (from Sesame Street) so I just loved him immediately, he's such a sweet warm person, so you have to get past the stories people tell you.

I remember one day in rehearsal, it was my first time - Mick was talking to Keith and Keith said "Oh come by the house for a BBQ and bring the kids" and Mick said "OK I'll be there" so Keith gave him a kiss and that was nice after thirty years of being together.

Darryl Jones wasn't so nervous just more hungry for success.

Darryl Jones

This is my first real rock n' roll gig, this is a little bit more meat and potatoes, basically lets just make this song feel good, it doesn't matter if the performance is pristine or perfect or anything like that, let's just make it feel good (his first rock n' roll gig is with the Stones).

The Voodoo Lounge is over two hundred feet wide and eighty feet deep and Mick Jagger works every inch of it. Charlie would prefer if he would at least stay in sight, he hates it when Mick disappears for a few songs.

Mick Jagger

I'm at a loss too when I'm two hundred feet away, I don't know what's going on, I have to watch him to know what the beat is, it's not anything to do with the music really at that point when I'm two hundred feet away, I can watch him go bap, so I know I'm in time. I'm hearing it but I'm hearing it delayed, so I have to have been singing in the front, I've done it for years, it's very tricky but I'm into it but it's got nothing to do with the music really or like playing rehearsal. I would say to everyone this is great in here but we better get out on that stage because it is nothing to do with it cos I've gotta be two hundred feet away singing Jumpin' Jack Flash, not right next to Keith the whole time in the same dopey little room somewhere.

I do a bunch of movements, its just the first night, I start doing some movements that I kinda worked out but I haven't perfectly memorised because there's twenty eight songs and each ones gotta move. But I don't remember, so I start off and think am I doing the right move and think oh no, I'm doing the wrong move, but I like doing new moves and then I revert to the old ones but I like doing new moves it keeps me fresh, otherwise I'd start doing what I did in 1965. But its for me that it counts, obviously the audience is really important but I get turned on before they can, if I can't get excited by it how can they?

People came in their thousands for the first show in New York on the Friday night. Many people had gone to the Woodstock Festival (the most chaotic festival in the history of rock music) but the Stones still pulled a sell out show. The New York , Giant Stadium show is now documented on video for all to see. Jerry Hall, Patti Hansen (Keith's wife) and Jo Wood all attended the New York show - proud to be the wives of the conquering English band. Traffic came to a standstill leaving New Jersey. Having braved the rain (fresh from Woodstock) the Stones kept the audience happy on the remaining nights.

THE PRESS REACTION?

R. Harrington
Washington Post

Much of the crowd was on its feet all night from the youthful abandon of 'All Down the Line', to the grungy cheekiness of Honky Tonk Woman, to the power-chording of 'Start Me Up'. From the start, the Stones signalled that there would be bows aplenty to the past, and the songs would be played with the urgency, venom, and strength that made them 80 breathtaking first time around.

John Sakamoto
Toronto Sun

The world's most, ahem, venerable band kicked off their 12th North American tour here last night with a defiant, in-your-face performance for a pumped up sell-out crowd of 55,000 at JFK Stadium.

Lisa Robinson
New York Post

The Rolling Stones kicked off their first World Tour in six years last night and proved that they still do that voodoo that only they do so well. ... Flares exploded, lights blazed. The air was electric, hot, humid. When all is said and done, there is nothing quite like the excitement, or the buzz, of a Stones stadium show.

The Stones went on to conquer these following towns leaving the American tour in a blaze of glory. After the US they were to tour in countries that they hadn't played in for years, these included Mexico, Argentina and Brazil. Chris Jagger (Mick's brother) accompanied the band in Argentina and wrote favourable reviews for the English Marie Claire magazine and then it was onto Japan.

AMERICAN TOUR DATES 1994

WASHINGTON DC	RFK Stadium	August 1, 3
BIRMINGHAM	Legion Field	August 6
INDIANAPOLIS	Hoosier Dome	August 10
NEW YORK	Giants Stadium	August 12, 14, 15, 17
TORONTO	Exhibition Stadium	August 19, 20
WINNIPEG	Winnipeg Stadium	August 23
MADISON	Camp Randall Stadium	August 26
CLEVELAND	Municipal Stadium	August 28
CINCINNATI	Riverfront Stadium	August 30
BOSTON	Foxboro Stadium	September 4, 5
RALEIGH	Carter Finley Stadium	September 7
EAST LANSING	Spartan Stadium	September 9
CHICAGO	Soldier Field	September 11, 12
DENVER	Mile High Stadium	September 15
COLUMBIA MO	Faurot Field	September 18
PHILADELPHIA	Veteran Stadium	September 22, 23
COLUMBIA SC	Brice Stadium	September 25
MEMPHIS	Liberty Bowl	September 27
PITTSBURGH	Three Rivers Stadium	September 29
AMES, IOWA	Cyclone Stadium	October 1
EDOMONTON	Commonwealth Stadium	October 4, 5
NEW ORLEANS	Superdome	October 10
LAS VEGAS	MGM Grand Garden	October 14, 15
SAN DIEGO	Jack Murphy Stadium	October 17
PASADENA LA	Rose Bowl	October 19, 21
SALT LAKE CITY	Mirage Stadium	October 23
OAKLAND	Alameda County	October 26, 28, 29, 31
EL PASO	University of Texas	November 3
SAN ANTONIO	Alamo Dome	November 5
LITTLE ROCK	War Memorial Stadium	November 11
HOUSTON	Astro Dome	November 13
ATLANTA	Georgia Dome	November 15, 16
DALLAS	Texas Stadium	November 18
TAMPA	Tampa Stadium	November, 22

MIAMI	Joe Robbie Stadium	November 25
GAINESVILLE	University of Florida	November 27
DETROIT	Silver Dome	December 1
TORONTO	Sky Dome	December 3
MONTREAL	Olympic Stadium	December 5, 6
SYRACUSE	Carrier Dome	December 8
MINNEAPOLIS	Metro Dome	December, 11
SEATTLE	King Dome	December 15
VANCOUVER	BC Place	December 17, 18

SOUTH AMERICAN TOUR DATES 1995

MEXICO	Mexico City	January 14, 16, 18
BRAZIL	San Paulo	January 27, 28
BRAZIL	Rio De Janeiro	February 2
ARGENTINA	Buenos Aires	February 4, 9, 11, 12, 14
SOUTH AFRICA	Johanesburg	February 24

東京ドーム公演オフィシャルエージェント
コンサート期間中、会員特別料金
都内ホテルの予約を受け付けます

BIG

東京ドームトラベルサービスでは、今回の東京ドーム公演オフィシャルエージェントとして、ローリング・ストーンズ日本公演にあわせて、東京都内のホテルをご用意しております。ローリング・ストーンズファンクラブの皆様の為の特別料金となっております。なお、当社でご用意できますお部屋数にも限りがございますので、コンサート終了後にご宿泊の予定をなさっています方は、**2月17日迄**にご予約下さい。

予約専用電話：**03-3817-6320**
受付時間：**10:00〜17:00**（土・日 祝祭日除く

＊ホテル名、ルームタイプ、ルーム料金、弊社へのお支払い方法など、詳細につきましては、上記の電話番号に
　問い合わせ下さい。

株式会社 東京ドームトラベルサービス   TOKYO DOME TRAVEL SERVICE CORPORAT

運輸大臣登録一般旅行業1035号／日本旅行業（JATA）正会員
〒112 東京都文京区後楽1-3　　TEL 03-3817-6150　FAX 03-3817-6

1995年NFLプロボウル観戦ハワイツアー／1995年2月2日（木）出

（NFLオールスター戦）
NFL公認オリジナルグッズプレゼント　　　　　　　　旅行 143,00

MOON IS UP

It took twenty eight years before the Stones were allowed into Japan, let alone play there. Previous drug related criminal offenses kept them out. What eventually swung it for the Stones was increasing public demand and the possibility of earning millions from the tour - finally the authorities agreed to a tour.

The *"Steel Wheels Tour"* broke all previous records in Tokyo, all six nights billed were sold out at The Tokyo Dome, a vast indoor arena usually used for baseball.

Although the Japanese seem withdrawn, when it came to the opening chords, everyone was on their feet leaving the pre-concert sushi boxes under their seats. Inside the Tokyo Dome itself the seats seem to go into the sky. In the seating only Dome, everyone is guided to their seats, the concert brought an ecstatic response from the crowd. After the encore the crowd were asked to be seated and were not allowed to leave until guided out in turn by the stewards.

The Steel Wheels concert in effect opened doors for the Stones individual members to undertake their own concerts in Japan, ranging from Mick Jagger's solo concert at the Tokyo Dome to Charlie Watts at Spiral Hall Jay concert also in Tokyo.

By the time the *"Voodoo Lounge Tour"* hit Japan they were familiar faces in the land of the rising sun. The unanimous verdict of the media and the audiences was that this was "The best rock 'n' roll show to hit the Far East".

JAPANESE TOUR DATES
TOKYO   *Tokyo Dome*   *March 6, 8, 9, 12, 14, 16, 17*
FUKUOKA   *March 22, 23*

-49-

MEET ME AT THE BOTTOM

The Stones have not toured in New Zealand since 1965, twenty nine years later had been a long interval.

The tour took the promoters by surprise, an extra show had to be added due to unprecedented ticket demand. Auckland the main city of New Zealand which holds a third of the total population of the country - one million - were relieved to know that they had not been forgotten on the World Tour map. Gered Mankowitz, whose marvellous photographs grace the Voodoo Lounge Catalogue, flew to New Zealand to promote his limited edition book featuring early photos of the Stones, which due to the euphoria surrounding the Rolling Stones Tour did very well. A well known phrase in the sixties and seventies "Would you let your daughter see the Rolling Stones", was well and truly put to bed, as mothers encouraged daughters not to miss out on an event of a lifetime like most of them had been forced to do.

The welcome and reaction in Australia was much the same the only difference being that they had seen the Stones on various tours since 1965. The usual amount of stubbies were drunk by correspondents and journalists in the hospitality tent and even after the 'stubbies' were consumed the general consensus was that it was the best band to hit Brisbane in a long time.

AUSTRALIAN & NEW ZEALAND TOUR DATES

AUSTRALIA	*Melbourne*	*March 27*
AUSTRALIA	*Sydney*	*April 1*
NEW ZEALAND	*Adelaide*	*April 5*
AUSTRALIA	*Perth*	*April 8*
AUSTRALIA	*Brisbane*	*April 12*
AUSTRALIA	*Aukland*	*April 16*
SINGAPORE		*April 21*

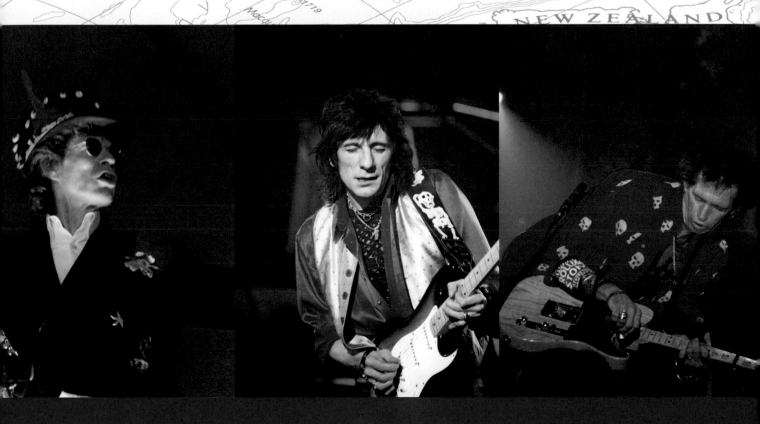

EUROPE

The tour was announced from Ronnie Wood's house in Dublin and it is amply equipped to supply Guinness on tap to any thirsty journalists.

The European leg of the tour had already gathered momentum before it had even begun. Sales had exceeded all expectations in the UK, Germany and Holland consequently extra dates were added to fulfil ticket demand.

EUROPEAN TOUR DATES

SWEDEN	Stockholm	Olympic Stadium	June 3
FINLAND	Helsinki	Olympic Stadium	June 6
NORWAY	Oslo	Vallehovin	June 9
DENMARK	Copenhagen	Parken	June 11
NETHERLANDS	Nujmegen	Park De Goffert	June 13, 14
NETHERLANDS	Landgraaf	Pinkpop Site	June 18
GERMANY	Cologne	Mungersdorfer	June 20
GERMANY	Hanover	Neidersachsen	June 22
BELGIUM	Werchter	Festival Site	June 24, 25
FRANCE	Paris	Longchamps	June 30, July 1
FRANCE	Paris	Olympia	July 3
UNITED KINGDOM	Sheffield	Don Valley Stadium	July 9
UNITED KINGDOM	London	Wembley Stadium	July 11, 15, 16
UNITED KINGDOM	London	Brixton Academy	July 19
SPAIN	Gijon	El Molinon	July 22
PORTUGAL	Lisbon	Alvalade Stadium	July 24
FRANCE	Montpellier	Grammont	July 27
SWITZERLAND	Basel	Jakob Stadium	July 29, 30
AUSTRIA	Zeltweg	Osterreich Ring	August, 1
GERMANY	Munich	Olympia Stadion	August 3
CZECH REPUBLIC	Prague	Strahov Stadium	August 5
HUNGARY	Budapest	Nepstadion	August 8
GERMANY	Schuttorf	Open Air	August 12
GERMANY	Leipzig	Festwiese	August 15
GERMANY	Berlin	Olympic Stadium	August 17
GERMANY	Hockenheim	The Ring	August 19
GERMANY	Mannheim	Maimarkt	August 22
LUXEMBOURG	Kirchberg	VW Gelande	August 25
NETHERLANDS	Rotterdam	Feynoord Stadium	August 29, 30
UNITED KINGDOM	London	Bagleys Warehouse	September 21

ITALY

Italy was omitted from the European tour due to the fact that their last tour *'The Steel Wheels'* tour in Rome was poorly attended, only 3,000 people arriving to witness the band play on Jaggers birthday. This was the only case where they hadn't sold out the tour and they didn't want to risk a repeat performance.

FRANCE

Having played in the pouring rain at the Stadium supported by Bon Jovi, the Stones decided to play at the Paris Olympia, July 3rd, to a stunned audience. They last played at this venue in 1966. The atmosphere said it all, it was going to be a special night. Jack Nicholson sat next to Jerry Hall up in the balcony. Mick's son threw water from the balcony onto the overheated crowd in the stalls, who had to endure an awful French support band for one hour. The band braved the abuse from the audience, stumbling off after one hour. The crowd went ecstatic the moment the Stones came on stage with Mick Jagger blowing a birthday kiss to his wife Jerry in the circle as Keith's father sat grinning with his pipe proud to be the father of the one and only living guitar legend.

This proved to be the best performance to date on the tour with the whole audience left awestruck at the diversity of the set. With numbers being played from *'Exile On Main Street'*, *'Shine A Light'* and other numbers culminating in *'Jumping Jack Flash'* with Bobby Keys keeping the power going to the last note. The Stones triumphed and then went off to celebrate Jerry Hall's birthday with Charlie Watts at a top French restaurant finally resting at the Georges Cinq Hotel. London still had to be conquered.

Monday July 3 1995
OLYMPIA

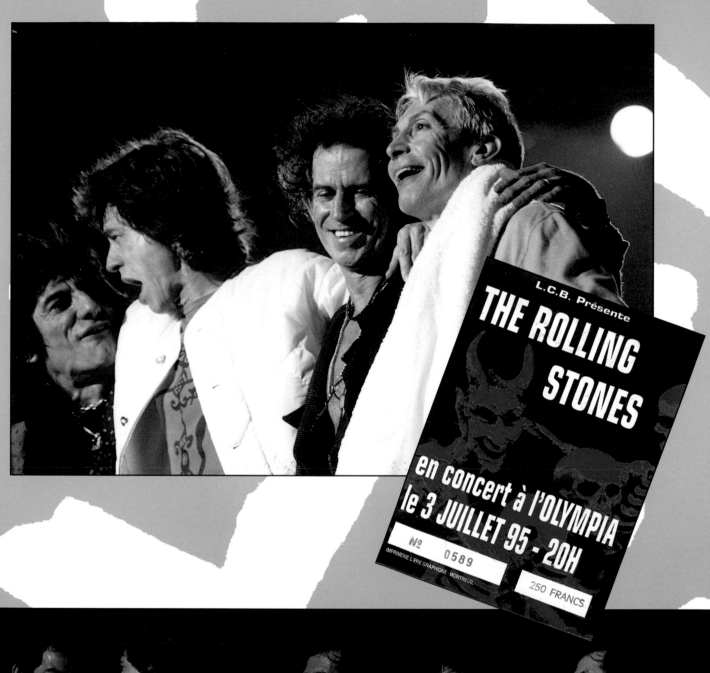

L.C.B. Présente
THE ROLLING STONES
en concert à l'OLYMPIA
le 3 JUILLET 95 - 20H
Nº 0589
IMPRIMERIE L'ERE GRAPHIQUE · MONTREUIL
250 FRANCS

THE UNITED KINGDOM

The Rolling Stones last played in the UK in 1992 *'The Urban Jungle Tour'*. A press conference was held at The Tabernacle in Powis Square, Notting Hill Gate, *'Performance'* was originally filmed here starring Jagger in 1969. Jagger and the press do not always see eye to eye, Jagger has often been accused of being arrogant. The paparazzi are always willing to sully someone's reputation, and sensationalism sells a few more copies of their newspapers and magazines. This occasion should have been no different but much to everyone's amazement they could only find praise for the tour, it's almost like an initiation ceremony, bands of such calibre and fame have to be publicly trashed before appreciation is forthcoming and it seems that history has only served to repeat itself for this tour.

Ticket sales were down and the touts/scalpers were selling £30 tickets for £5 before the show on Tuesday at Wembley Stadium. By Sunday night however, the excellent reviews and the somewhat delayed exuberant response to the concerts, made the demand for the tickets unprecedented. Wembley has a capacity for 70,000, to illustrate the point, £25 standing only tickets were being brought by the touts for the remaining concerts for £35 and the few tickets that they had access to were being sold for £70 and rising.

Ronnie Wood could be heard saying "I'm enjoying the tour, as the press can't wait to say The Stones are past it only to be proven wrong".

The selection of merchandise has never been so varied, telephone cards, credit cards, spiky tongue badges to name but a few, as well as bootleg merchandise which was quite prolific.

Backstage at the concert, the Voodoo Lounge consisted of the usual smattering of Rolling Stones wannabees, leading to the sycophantic ramblings of all and sundry determined on claiming the Stones as best mates. Unlike other rock legends, The Stones as individuals keep their distance from anyone other than their immediate family and a few close friends and thus refrained from attending the Voodoo Lounge on the last night.

As usual the Stones played alternate tracks on the three nights varying from Heartbreaker on Saturday night to Happy on Sunday night.

The Wembley concert finished in an explosion of fireworks and Japanese music as the ecstatic crowd piled out of the Stadium. There was a definite buzz in the air aside from the euphoria the crowd was feeling after the concert ,this had been created by Mick Jagger's final words on stage "See you in Brixton". It seemed that the best rock n' roll band in the world had another chapter to add to their world tour.

BRIXTON, England

On Tuesday morning 18th July The Brixton Academy gig was going to became a reality for many fans. To see the artists they idolised in such close proximity was a dream come true. However, before it was made official, there was only hearsay and rumour to content oneself with, but then word got out that Virgin Megastore in London were going to sell 2,500 on Tuesday morning at 10.00am. Fans started queuing at 7pm Monday night, prepared to wait the night out to ensure that they were first in line to secure a ticket to the most coveted Stones gig of the tour. By 5.00 am Tuesday morning the queue had grown to humongous proportions, Stones fans in good humour and extremely well behaved had formed a line going straight past the front door of Vinyl Experience on Hanway Street and the nether regions of the queue were trailing in Charing Cross Road.

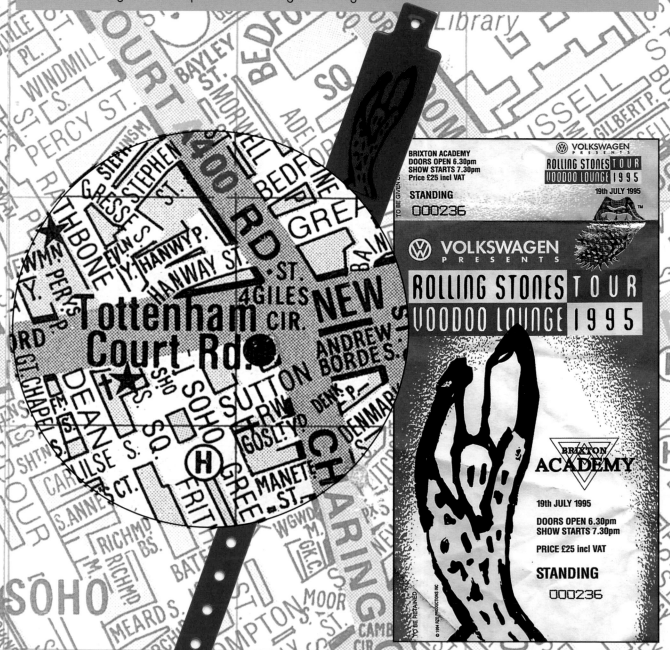

The bargain price of £25 was paid for standing only tickets on the sloping ground floor of Brixton Academy (capacity 4,000) with the all seating tickets upstairs going to celebrities such as Mick Hucknall, Marianne Faithful who earlier on in the same day signed copies of her most recent book commented "Not tonight darling" in her perfect English accent as a fan asked her for her autograph. Mick's family were present as well as Michael Hutchence (of INXS fame) accompanied by Bob Geldof's other half and Bob Geldof himself - gasp!   Earlier on in the day Darryl Jones had rehearsed in his room at the Regency Hotel, new tracks that were to be played later that night including a great acoustic set recorded for the new album *'Stripped'* included classics such as *'Faraway Eyes'*, a stomping version of the old blues classic *'Meet Me At The Bottom'* and *'Angie'* to name but a few.

Nancy Berry of Virgin Records whose husband runs Radio One (surely a conflict of interest), masterminded the recording of the concert, telling MTV who thought they owned the name "unplugged" in the nicest possible way that she was recording the concert and promptly having done so tried to sell the show back to MTV to broadcast. They refused the show saying they were not interested having been blown out in the first place.... The final episode of the tour occurred on September 20th with a party, filmed for the video, at the Grosvenor Hotel followed by an impromptu live performance at 4.00pm in Kings Cross the following day, September 21st - always a band to surprise the public.

Picture: DAVE HOGAN

Sweat and Satisfaction

RONNIE WOOD and Mick Jagger enjoyed another hot and triumphant night as the Rolling Stones abandoned their multi-million pound Voodoo Lounge stage set to rock a steamy Brixton Academy in front of just 3,000 fans and 800 guests. *Full story: Page 6*

Hot stuff as no-frills Stones rock Brixton

THE NIGHT was hot, the walls were dripping sweat and Brixton felt like New Orleans. Conditions were perfect for the Rolling Stones.

And suddenly there was Keith Richards, crouched at the front of the Academy stage, grinding out the opening chords we'd all heard a thousand times before, and the Stones were on stage, playing Honky Tonk Women. This time you could actually see them: no video screen necessary. You could even see the lines on Mick Jagger's face, though that's the only thing that betrayed his age as he ran and leapt and strutted and pouted like a man 30 years younger.

It was as if the clock had been turned back as the Stones went back to their roots to play the music that inspired them in the early Sixties for a crowd of just 3,000 fans and 800 friends and guests, who included Jagger's wife Jerry Hall, George Harrison, Mick Hucknall, Joe Strummer, Duran Duran and Michael Hutchence.

If the Stones weren't having fun they must be phenomenal actors, whatever their critics might say. In the middle of Live With Me, Mick paused to mop Keith's brow as he hammered out the chords, then ran to the side of the stage to slap palms with the crowd.

Richards and Ronnie

by TIM COOPER

Wood demonstrated the art of formation cigarette smoking, while the backing singers synchronised thigh slaps.

Bob Dylan's Like A Rolling Stone was the show-stopper it was at Wembley, or "the big place" as Jagger referred to the stadium, and the crowd went berserk.

The set's closing numbers, Start Me Up and Brown Sugar, sent the audience even crazier before the Stones returned for the finale of Jumping Jack Flash. The roar of approval was unanimous on a night the Stones proved they don't need the £15 million stage set, the inflatables and video screens. After 33 years, they still do it best on their own.

My wildlife as a Rolling Stone: Page 19

ROTTERDAM

The final concert in Rotterdam, Holland was filled to the brim. The fans realising this was to be the final concert of this two year tour flocked in their thousands to witness another Stadium show. The Stones never a band to disappoint their fans played an extra half hour on top of their two hour show. The finale ended with the fireworks exploding, the fans soaking wet from the constant downpour left ecstatic - their personal saving put to good use as they toured around the world to witness their band - the peoples band. Many of the fans witnessed over fifty shows on the Voodoo Lounge Tour, never tiring of any one of them.

The Stones are the only rock 'n' roll band to have spanned over four decades teenagers all over the world have grown up with them and for many it has become a way of life carrying the Stones with them into adulthood and following them like pilgrims on various tours. Most fans will remember exactly where they were and what they were doing for the Stones gigs for example the infamous concert held in 1969 - Hyde Park, and in fact most fans will relate events to each different gig they have been to right from the very beginning, it is literally a way of life.

NOT FADE AWAY

The Stones themselves don't know where it will end but they have some words to impart.

Keith Richards

It's too late for job training we've got to keep the thing going.
I've never felt rebellion, you are or you ain't. In the sixties there was a need to be rebellious, you had a generation growing up in the aftermath of World War 2 and suddenly in the sixties it was time to change a few things. Hitler was on my tail he dropped a bomb on my bed, I was six months old. My mum had taken me out while she was buying some black market nylons in town, we came back and it was one of those flying bombs and it had landed right in my bed. Still we saw him off - we fixed that. The fifties were trying to recover and all I can remember is rubble and it was like that for years. I grew up during the recovery and suddenly for my generation the music went from black and white to technicolour and it was just what we needed.

Another reason for the length of time the band has been together is friendship.

Mick Jagger

Friendship has to be in the equation sometimes, it's very volatile and fragile, so if you just have a professional relationship with people, you don't have any of those problems.

Mick and Keith are classed as hard businessmen with Keith being Mr Nice Guy.

Keith Richards

Yes we play up to it a bit, I suppose there is an element of truth in it as well, me, I enjoy the highs and lows, Mick doesn't like his feathers ruffled. But what Mick and I do know is who is the best person to handle the situation, time for Mr Smoothy pants or unleash the tiger, we use whatever is appropriate and we're good at it.

Ronnie Wood

We're the only pioneers in rock n' roll even though I am the new boy of twenty years, they have set a precedent which only the old blues boys had done they worked until they dropped on stage and I think that's what we'll probably do.

Whether it goes on for a year and a half or twelve years, I don't want it to stop.

One of the first times I ever met Keith was when Mick and Bianca were getting married in Biblos in the South of France, so we've been a team since May 1971.

We were in Montserrat recording 'Steel Wheels' and that went very well and we all felt the first gear of the new Rolling Stones skipping into shape and each gig got better and better. It was a sad situation when the tour wound down.

Keith Richards
It's too early to tell about a legacy, you don't start out doing this to influence people necessarily but there is a point where you realise you're a voice for a generation where you shake it up and suddenly you wonder if you designed it or not or if you just felt an obligation to do what your doing.

I don't think you can take up rock 'n' roll at fifty and then suddenly realise that youth has a lot to do with it. As long as you can start young who knows what your limits will be and how long you can take it, we grew up with this stuff.

It's a misconception that you have to be a teenager or in your twenties to do it, otherwise we wouldn't be here. Other guys can take this up for a living too, its not just something that you take up at the age of twenty five, as long as your good at it, age doesn't matter.

Charlie Watts
I play in a band and I enjoy it and I've been doing it for years and at the moment I enjoy it. We have been doing this for a long time and we have a lot of very professional people around us and regardless of what you think of us, we are professional. Keith Richards has never missed a show ever, I've only missed one because I forgot the day and that's professionalism, headaches, hangovers, nothing stands in the way and that's what we do.

Keith Richards
I met Mick in a sand pit when we were four years old, but at the same time we are different people, I know exactly what you mean and that is what I mean about chemistry. In a normal course of events, Mick, Charlie and I probably would never have met. There's some strange threads that personality wise it balances out into the weirdest mixture, but bands are always like that actually.

SWEETHEARTS TOGETHER

No professional band has survived intact playing continuously for thirty four years. Even after this historic duration the Stones are not finished, as long as the record buying public keep buying their music and the fans keep coming to see them, they will be around for a while yet. Three generations have grown up with the Stones and it is set to continue. They have flown the English flag endlessly it seems and they still have nothing to show for it from the Queen. They are renowned world-wide, everyone knows the Stones.

Blues artists such as Muddy Waters are legends in their own right but the Stones are a band, not an individual, so in a way their achievement of being together for thirty-four years is even more remarkable.

The tour has ended but for 1996 there are more surprises to come.